Georgia Sketch Book

TEXT AND DRAWINGS BY

Ouida Canaday

PEACHTREE PUBLISHERS, LIMITED
Atlanta, Georgia

Published by
PEACHTREE PUBLISHERS, LTD.
494 Armour Circle, N. E., Atlanta, Georgia 30324

Copyright © 1981 Ouida Canaday

Manufactured in the United States of America

First edition

Library of Congress Catalog No. 81-84168
ISBN: 0-931948-29-0

Dedicated To
Betty Foy Sanders,
Who taught me to
Love Georgia!

Ouida
Canaday

As I sit on my folding stool, making yet another sketch of a kudzu covered tenant house whose former occupants now live in a city condominium, it occurs to me that I've been watching and painting this land and its good folks for almost thirty years – and yet I feel as though I'm just beginning. Many years ago I married a Georgia Cracker who was born on the Nowhere Road in the Sawdust Community. It was then that I became aware that Georgia was more than miles and miles of red clay and slash pine between my native Florida and the rest of the world. It was much later that I discovered the best kept secret in the fifty states. On a cold day in Georgia I can ski in the morning, and gather shells on the shores of the Atlantic the same afternoon! I can safely stroll down a shaded street in a friendly rural town, and one hour later be hurled by a spectacular expressway into one of the most progressive cities in the world. The "Happy Darkie," symbolic a few years back of the romantic, historical South, now participates in the legislature, runs City Hall, and among other things signficiantly figures in our booming recording industry. The Good Ol' Boy has become as well known in Washington and Wall Street as in the backwoods and country store at home. When he does return, he exchanges the Brooks Brothers look for a well worn pair of designer jeans, hops in the pickup with gunrack and faithful coon dog, to tear up the country roads doing whatever Good Ol' Boys do best. The Chameleon Southland continues to make an inexhaustible, provocative subject for creative minds to write and paint about. As I look back at the old farm house, once new and modern-seeming to its builders, I find it interesting to contemplate the inevitable possibility that things we consider as progressive in our day — that pride of the Expressway System, The Cloverleaf, for instance — may one day seem as quaint and picturesque as this old house.

Who in the world can be knocking at this time of night? I don't know anyone up here! I open the door to find a young mountain man looking at me. "You the Paintin' Lady?" I nod. . . . Into the darkness he shouts, "It's okay, Paw. This is her!" Paw, Maw, Son, Grandmaw, Grandpaw, four kids, two neighbors, and a coon dog enter. Expressionless faces quietly scan the thirty-some-odd works I have completed over the past two weeks. It's a strange gallery — paintings and drawings lean against the walls, hang on door knobs, perch on sink and refrigerator. A light appears in Grandpaw's eye. He heads for a drawing of a swayback, tumbledown house; they all gather 'round to inspect it in silence. Then, softly, "I was borned in that house. . . ." The silence broken, the generations begin to identify, with politely muted exclamations of recognition, various buildings, streams, and fields. Next morning, I find on my front porch a mess-of-beans, six vineripe tomatoes, and two jars of crabapple jelly.

I've never found anyone more pleasant to converse with than this lovely, hundred-year-old mountain lady. The tales she spins are so engaging that I'm sorry I can listen only with my half an ear while I concentrate on her portrait. "I came to this valley when I was a girl of fourteen. While my man built the cabin, we lived in a lean-to made of wood stuck together with clay. At first we had only three walls and a roof. On cold winter nights the wild varmints would come in and share our fire. We never knew what we'd find curled up on the hearth in the morning." She tells of the dozen children that survived out of the twenty-two she gave birth to, and recounts how she clothed them with the wool she sheared from her sheep — carding, spinning, and knitting it into warm garments. . . . My hostess has heard all about Grandma Moses, one of the artists featured on her last year's calendar. She assures me that someday, if I get good enough, maybe I'll have a picture on a calendar, too. My friend's daughter (in her eighties!) has gone out with her shovel to dig up a mountain plant I admired earlier. I don't know how I'll get it home, but somehow I will, and every time I look at it planted in my own yard, I'll remember this day as a Gift of Love.

It's no easy trick getting all my sketching gear up the trail and out on this rock in the midst of a torrent of rushing, white water. All around me are waterfalls of all sizes, talking to each other, and to me. I thought it would be quiet and peaceful here, but there is nothing peaceful about tons of power racing down a mountain, crashing against giant boulders, and sculpting the earth to its own demands. If I want peace, I'll have to find one of the quieter pools further downstream where you can hear the birds call to one another. In the mysterious shadows of the tangled mountain laurel on these slopes, I imagine I see a doe – probably only wishful thinking, but in this magic place, daydreams could become realities. I wonder how long that giant hemlock stood before some villain tore it from the ground and cast it into the torrent. Was it lightning? Or was it the river itself? I start to use the rock I'm sitting on as a pallet for mixing my paints, but decide not to disturb the rich velvety gray-green lichen that so generously provides me with a cushion. The whole world

is misty green and gray, but mostly white – even the roaring sound seems a searing white. A shaft of sunlight suddenly penetrates my secret place to cast a handful of diamonds on the water before me. My hand is too slow . . . my pallet inadequate. Why do I always attempt the impossible? Oh, well, the original Artist didn't do it all in one day, either.

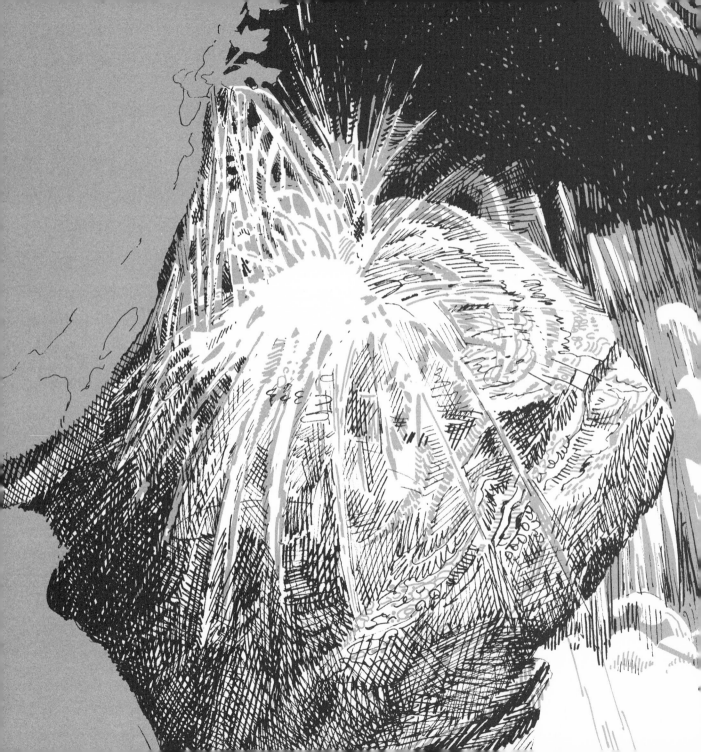

Five miles of marble quarry lie before me, and here I've chosen a shadeless spot to work from. What a sight! It reminds me of a Pre-Columbian dig. How can I possibly capture its grandeur in my small sketch book? . . . Now, an hour or two later, the sun has caught up with me and I'm about to roast! What I wouldn't give for a shade tree! From this distance, the workmen in the quarry look like toys. They know I'm sketching them – one of them looked in this direction, then stopped work to comb his hair. Oh, oh! I got permission to sketch here, but it looks like I'm in someone's way. Two men are rolling an enormous cable spool across the field toward me, and two more are dragging a large cottonwood tree. I'd better pack my gear. Well, I'm finished anyway, and it will be great to find a nice cool place. "Good day, ma'am. We noticed how hot you are and thought you might like some shade." The cable spool is laid on its side and the cottonwood placed in the hole in its middle – instant shade! "How thoughtful of you. This is great! Now I can really do a good job. Goodbye!" I guess I'm going to have to sit here for a while longer to show my appreciation. . . . Oh, well, I can always draw the cottonwood.

It never ceases to amaze me how interested the whole world seems in the mystique of making art. I once had a family of palomino horses peer over my shoulder for awhile as I worked, then prance over to kick the bejeebers out of my styrofoam ice chest! I re-examined my painting and decided the horses were absolutely right — it was pretty awful. Speaking of art critics, here comes Farmer Brown. "Hi there!" I greet him. "The lady up at the house said it was all right for me to sketch here." Silence. (I'm making what is known as a "gesture drawing" — broad, loose sweeping motions to catch the "rhythm" of land, buildings and trees. It looks like a long dropped tangle of fishing line.) "Is the lady at the house your wife?" "Un, huh." A half hour later the tangled line has begun to take form. "Do you own all this land?" "Uh, huh." I wish I could get him to pose for me. Marvelous nose and cheek bones. Great strong hands. "Did you build the rock chimney and split the rails for the fence?" "Uh, huh." That takes care of another half hour's conversation. The trees in my drawing now grow out of the ground, and the buildings look cared for. I tear the page from my sketch book and hand it to him. For a long while he doesn't speak or move.

Then in awed amazement, "You done that with your hands!" This from a man who has just realized that hands are used for more than building barns, splitting rails, and making rock chimneys.

What a sight for sore eyes – yard chickens! I have just about come to the conclusion that folks don't have yard chickens any more. Automatic feeders serve thousands of chickens their every need – automatic daylight, automatic music, automatic everything. Why, when I was a girl, even city folks had yard chickens. A friend of mine was given a family of Bantams one Christmas and he let them run loose all over the neighborhood. I remember we had a hammock that summer and it was my favorite place to be. I used to lure the "Bantys" under the hammock with bits and pieces of my peanut butter and jelly sandwich. One day I noticed that the chickens were definitely communicating with one another. I imitated the sounds they made and found to my delight that they were indeed having a conversation! Soon I was able to "talk chicken" well enough to say, "Look out, everybody, here comes a hawk!" or, "Hey, gang! I've found a peanut butter and jelly sandwich big enough to feed the whole family!" To the embarrassment of some of my friends, and the pleasure of others, I  have experimented with my chicken vocabulary all over the world. I find the sounds are universal. The lady who lives in this house thought it strange when I asked to sketch her chickens. I've noticed two very inquisitive eyes peering at me through a slightly parted curtain. I wonder how she's going to react when I start talking to them!

I was searching for a spot on the river where I was told the local people have their Baptisings. Instead, I've gotten lost trying to take a short cut through these dense woods. I finally find a deer trail leading me to a sunny clearing. In the middle is a fine two story Victorian house. I notice there are no roads leading to this spot except the path that brought me here! The doors and windows stand open, the decorative gingerbread trim is unbroken. If there are birds nesting within, there is no evidence. Vines and kudzu are curiously absent. I remember how many wonderful old Southern homes are said to be haunted and reassure myself that I don't believe such stories. Though aware of the danger of crime lurking even in isolated places, I feel compelled to go inside. Oddly, the hinges don't squeak as I push the door open. I move into the semidarkness and call out, "Anybody here?" Empty houses usually have a hollow sound. This one doesn't. As I walk from room to room I am impressed by the loving attention to detail in the craftsmanship of the construction. Upstairs, on a bedroom wall, I discover a large bevelled mirror, the only remaining furniture. For a moment I am stunned by my own image. Suddenly, I know I am unwelcome here. As

I run down the steps to the front door, my hand touches the beautiful carved railing and a chill races up my spine — there is no dust anywhere! I am now sitting in the sun, sketching from a safe and comfortable distance. As I look at the strange, lonely house, I get the peculiar impression . . . that the house . . . is watching me. . . .

She was a handsome, healthy seventy years and she had, all by herself, cut the six-foot tree from land that her father had cleared with an axe almost a century ago. She had brought it in and trimmed it with her own two hands. She lives alone with "Dog," who is supposed to take care of her, but because her old friend has arthritis, she takes care of him. Her face lights up when she reminisces about the man with the axe who cleared the land, built the house, and governed, with an iron hand, his enormous family. Such was his powerful influence that he might have been present at the Christmas feast his daughter served at the magnificent dining table he had carved from a poplar tree many years before. Had he actually been here, though, he would have found a few surprises — gas logs in his lovely fireplace, a color television, and a huge, double-door freezer filled with fruits and vegetables still grown on his own land. Georgia pioneers of agriculture, like this one, left their mark upon children, grandchildren, and great grandchildren alike, and laid the foundation upon which is built the Georgia we know today. During holidays, the neighboring farmhouses, some still occupied by family elders, have broomswept yards filled with cars bearing license tags from far and wide — relatives home for Christ-

mas. Sons and daughters, sent to the city for an education, stayed to become professional and business people, carrying with them the rich heritage of the stern settlers of the land. Because of their exodus, a new kind of farm has emerged. The once-picturesque fields are now crawling with mechancial monsters whose operators commute to work from comfortable homes in nearby towns. The young who do make an attempt to follow in granddad's footsteps recall with pride how he defended his crops with a shotgun from the government agent who came with the order to plow them under. The agent never came back and the crops were saved. These young families bring to the landscape the long, shiny mobile home which is rapidly replacing the shingle roofed farm house with the fieldstone chimney. Somehow I'm glad that the old man with the axe didn't live to see his world change from farm hand to mechanic . . . from the scent of hickory smoke to the smell of diesel oil. His worst fears were of epidemics, drought, and the erosion of top soil, creating canyons out of good farm land. Still, he knew that he and God together could conquer anything. We will never know how the giants of our past would have dealt with the present, but I'm mighty glad they were there to start us off on the right foot.

My friend, the Happy Woodcarver, has invited me to go with him into the "Land of the Trembling Earth" to hunt wood for his talented hands, his cleverly adapted dentist's tools. As we walk through ankle deep leaves, pushing a stick ahead of us to scare away snakes, this philosopher tells me that snakes, in their own habitat, are not dangerous. "When at home, they know the escape routes and would rather run away than hurt you." He searches for wood that already has "Swamp Critters" inside, recognizes them, and cuts away the extra wood to let the critters out. He installs me on a fallen tree that hangs out over the water, and goes on his way to meet his swamp friends. I'm alone with giant cypress, waterlilies, and . . . no! I'm not alone! There, below my dangling feet, is a water snake, gracefully skimming across the red-black water. . . . Animal and insect sounds have increased, and a crystal dragonfly has joined me on my private log. A big, fat frog is in danger of becoming Mister Moccasin's

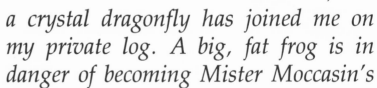

*dinner. Nearby I see a giant pray-
ing mantis. There's something
human about the way she turns
her eyes to look back at me. . . .
I'm almost sorry when The Woodcarver returns and interrupts my
collecting of new and delightful
impressions. Back at the parking lot, while unloading his
croker sack full of wood into the car trunk, he quietly
commands, "Ouida! Don't move!" Respecting his stern
order, I freeze. He reaches into the back of his belt for his
axe, and with one swift motion, decapitates a large water
moccasin coiled to strike. For a few seconds he stares down
at the dying creature, then sadly, "Son, you had no business being away from home. . . ."*

It's a good thing it rained today, otherwise I would still be sitting out there under a moss-draped oak, recording nature, defying five-foot moccasins, Russian wild boar, and even larger mosquitos. Usually the jeep puts me out in the morning at the Wild Things' favorite watering hole, and picks me up later in the day. Somehow, throwing sticks at snakes slithering across the dead leaves has become a natural reflex. Today, with rain pounding on the tin roof of my makeshift studio, I'm trying to put it all together. Artists are gatherers, and this Golden Isle is a supermarket of sensuous goodies. I have gathered the skull of a deer, spectacular shells, and driftwood, but mainly I've been gathering, with my other four senses, the sounds and scents of a tropical island almost untouched by modern civilization. Add to this the taste of freshly caught shrimp, boiled in beer, and the touch of damp moss on my cheek. My head is buzzing with rhythms and notes that make up the song of nature. The same rhythm pattern permeates the moss, tides, dunes, the drumming of the rain, all keeping time with the island itself. I've put away clocks and have no idea how long I've been painting this day, but I feel satisfied. I don't know yet if my painting is any good – it's too soon – I do know that the act of painting was good! Usually I destroy my bad canvases, but this one, good or bad, I will always treasure, because it's a collection of precious moments which can never be repeated.

As soon as the light comes in the east, I'm awake and on the beach. I've never been a Beach Bum, but if I ever become one, this is the beach I'd like to "Bum" on! Shells are abundant, and so are Shell People. Shell People carry a plastic bag or a bucket, walk slowly, head lowered, gaze focused at their feet, oblivious to crashing surf, roaring jet, or screaming children – poised to pounce upon some rare find before another Shell Person (the Enemy) spots and challenges ownership. A genuine Shell Person watches with relief as a sunbrowned body jogs on by without even glancing down – one less competitor for the "good stuff." I've seen the Shell Game turn lifelong friends into deadly

enemies as they tugged away at a large conch which was seen simultaneously. They declared a frosty truce, but never again went to the beach together. Requirements for being a Shell Person are simple: a paperback Shell Book education, a timetable of the tides, and an alarm clock (so you can be the first one there when the tide leaves behind new treasures). Extraordinary patience and perseverance usually accompany Shell Fever. You may have guessed by now that I know all about Shell People because I am one — and Heaven help you if you get in my way when I spot a large conch!

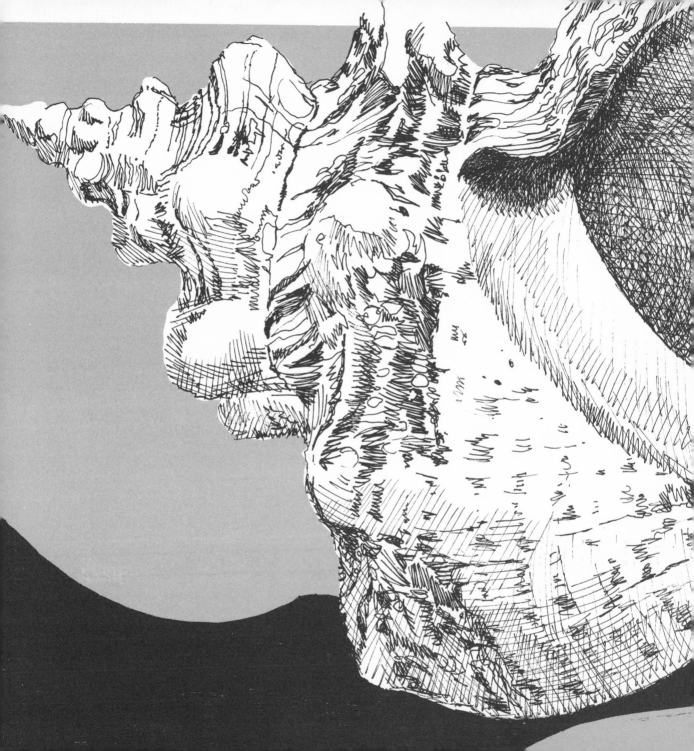

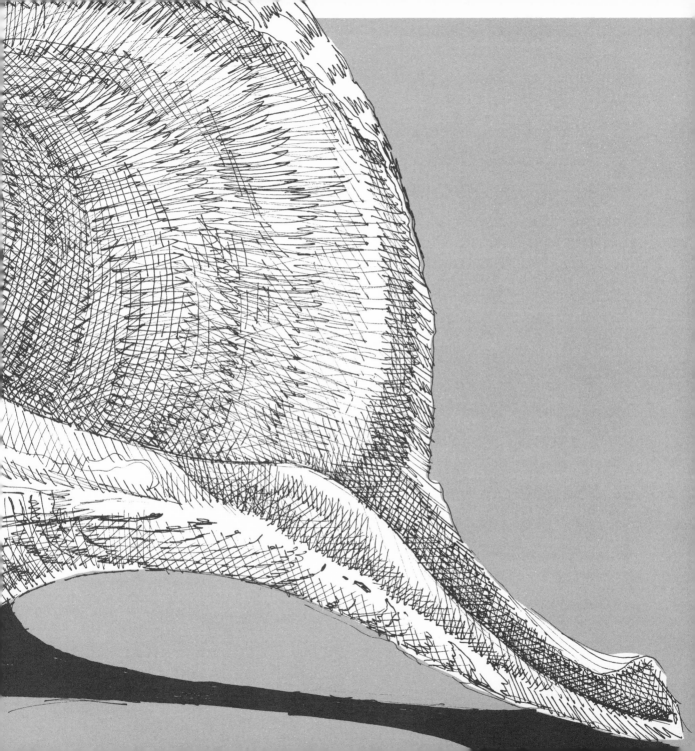

Spring has come to Georgia, and I have joined the birds in celebrating! They celebrate with song – my song is my sketch book. Whatever happened to that dull Georgia of my childhood – the Georgia I impatiently ignored on my way to other places? Its earth now seems richer and redder, one of the most beautiful colors I've ever seen! Now, wherever I travel in the world, my heart gives a tug if I see red clay, and I find myself thinking jealously, "What is my Georgia clay doing here?" Slash pines are filled with tiny yellow butterflies that I never noticed before. Were they always there? Today I discovered a sweetshrub. I'm told that grandmother crushed a piece of it in her hankie instead of using French perfume! Where was it when I was growing up? And how about the delicious, eatable pink of the peach blossoms, saturating the land for a few precious moments in spring, before the trees get down to work making peaches so we can call ourselves "The Peach State"? Were the dogwood and redbud, the Joe Pye weed and trillium always there? And if so, where was I???

Sources of Inspiration

Monticello
Waycross
Atlanta
Plains
Albany
Sky Valley
Columbus
Ellijay
Amacalola Falls
Anna Ruby Falls
Unicoi
Tate

Ballground
Gainesville
Savannah
Macon
Brunswick
Cuthbert
Providence Canyon
Okeefenokee Swamp
Ossabaw Island
Darian
Sea Island
Augusta

Griffin